You can skip this boring bit
(but it's legally necessary).

I0473493

WARNING

This book uses foul language, not out of choice, but
to provide definitions currently used in the prison
systems in Australia (including youth detention).

Contact details:

kurtreiter@mac.com

ISBN and re-sale details: refer to Amazon and the
back cover.

Table of Contents:

Chapter One: Assessment

I went to a number of male prisons in Victoria so have to admit I don't have personal experiences to comment on female prisons, federal prisons or interstate prisons but I have done a lot of research since my release and it would appear that they're all pretty similar.

In Victoria, you arrive at the "MAP" – a Melbourne based Assessment Prison where you will be in the mix of any sort of prisoner; be they sex offenders, murderers, junkies, dealers, white collar thieves and you are required to surrender your clothes, get your prison 'greens', have your first strip search and then have a shower before being interviewed by a number of Doctors and other people who are supposed to make sure you don't get harmed by food allergies and the like.

More on that later.

The strip search, if you've never had
become routine but at first is pret'

For men, the process is as fo)'

(a) take your clothes off in front of an Officer;

(b) run your fingers through your hair;

(c) pull both ears back, one at a time;

(d) put your arms out so your armpits can be viewed;

(e) lift your penis and lift up your testicles: what the Officers refer to as "tackle";

(f) turn around;

(g) lift your feet, one at a time, wiggle your toes; and

(h) split your cheeks so that they can check there is nothing hidden in your arse.

For women, my understanding is that is the same process with the exception that rather than do a 'tackle' check you need to bend over to the point where the Officer can see both your arse and vagina the same time, whether or not you have your iod.

Depending on your 'status' this can be done daily or every few days. The good news is that after a while you just get you used to it. As someone who was always very private I've become used to the fact that people might see me naked – it's one of the few many interesting things that I learnt from being in prison.

Of course, then there is the compulsory piss test. These happen in every prison on a regular basis.

Both measures are designed to stop drugs getting into prison; which seems reasonable but I've got a lot more to tell you about that later on if you made it this far.

Chapter Two: Lingo

If this is going to be your first time inside, this is probably the most important thing you will ever read in your entire life.

There is a language that exists in both male and female prisons Australia wide and if you don't know it in advance – you're in for the shock of your life and the strip searches and urine tests will seem irrelevant by comparison. And if you don't know them in advance you will be quickly determined as a first timer or in prison terms: "fresh meat".

The most significant terms are:

Cunt

A Cunt is a prisoner – you. It may seem strange but depending on your 'cunt' level, it can actually be helpful.

Screw

An officer is a 'screw' who is never to be trusted and being seen to assist them with anything will get you into trouble with other cunts, very quickly. So whilst most screws might be decent people you need to avoid them in anyway possible.

Lagging

Dobbing someone in to a screw for something you don't like, whether right or wrong, makes you a 'lagger'. Lagging in prison is the one of most serious breaches of what is known as the "cunt code" and if you lag on someone to a Screw you are going to pay a heavy price – everything from being beaten up (badly) to being murdered.

Cellies

These are your cell mates.

Dogs

Dogs are the term used for both the worst type of screws and sex offenders. Sex offenders have their own prison blocks know as "Protection".

Top Cunt

The top cunt is the most influential inmate in any prison. It won't take you long to work out who that is. And whomever it is – you befriend him or her as fast as you can because when trouble breaks out (which it will) he or she will sort it out.

Even the screws tend to avoid to the top cunt because within a click of a finger their would be a riot.

Smart Cunt

This is what I was referred because I could read and write letters for other Cunts. In fact; that's how I made it out alive: I was of use so I was protected by the Top Cunt without having to pay for it.

Shit Cunt

This is a lagger or someone who is nice to the screws and/or steals your canteen items. Shit cunts often do what is called a "professional bail" to have them isolated (slotted) because they know their life is at risk.

Crumb

If you are called a 'crumb' then you are considered worse than a shit cunt or even a dog. Crumbs are the worst and if you end up with that label, you can expect a lot of problems and expect to spend most of your sentence in the slot.

Throwing a Dirty

This is a failed piss test – if you've been taking drugs and got pinched, likely lagged on by the screw who you paid to get you the drugs and that's why you were targeted – so the price goes up.

The Slot

I've already referred to the "slot" which is an isolation cell – more to come on that if you continue to read on.

Mainstream

If you are playing 'nicely' you will be allowed to mix with other cunts between lock downs, your allocated work and counts, sometimes known as musters, where you can mix with others, visit the library, maybe read a newspaper, go for a walk, go to a gym, wash your clothes, see a Doctor and the like.

Mainstream is better than being in a slot but only if you have something to offer.

The most significant problem with mainstream is that you will, most likely have to share a cell.

I've written this short book in a way to avoid personal issues and politics but if you want to see politics in action – wait to see what happens when you have a cellie, be it one, two or more.

For most of the day, you have to sleep or spend time in your cell with a cellie, whether or not that cellie has anything in common with you or not.

You will have to agree, or succumb, to which TV shows to watch and at what times.

You will have to get used to the fact that you have to shit and shower in front of each other and come to terms over where you store your toiletries and if you're new then you're on one of the top bunks, irrespective of your age and medical needs.

If your cellie is a Violent Offender (VO) or a Serious Violent Offender (SVO) then don't expect to sleep much – you can expect TVs and plastic chairs to be thrown around in the middle of the night for no reason.

But even with all those risks and issues, I personally found mainstream to be more humane than the slot. At least you will get some social interaction – just be careful as to whom you make friends with.

Gear

This just means drugs.

Boss

Boss is a cunt term for 'Bucket of Steaming Shit' and the screws know that so you might think calling a screw Boss is being respectful but before you know it you're in the slot without even knowing why.

This happened to me.

Bronzing

When a cunt wants to make a silent protest, there are not too many options so one often used is using your own shit and smear it all over your body. This is mostly used to avoid court hearings but it will see you put in the slot and not before a Judge.

Kangaroo Court

If a screw doesn't like your attitude they can have you internally 'charged' with an offence – whether or not you committed it or not. There is no Court, no Judge, no Jury and the 'hearing' is conducted by a General Manager, a Governor or someone else appointed by the GM.

If you admit to the charge, you might avoid being slotted and you will get money deducted from your account. If you don't things will get nasty but you still shouldn't. That stated; either way: you have no control over anything and no one cares whether you did do something wrong or not, whether there is evidence or not and all you need to do to end up in a Kangaroo Court is piss off a screw.

Remember – the screws have no oversight. They can do whatever they like – there are no votes in prisoner rights so those charged to look after you don't care.**Jacks**

Jacks are simply the term for the Police.

Pinched

When you got caught by the Jacks or found guilty in Court.

Stood over

This is when your belongings are taken away from you by another cunt or cunts because you appear weak. No matter how scared you are – you must never give even the slightest hint that you are scared of anyone, no matter your size, weight, looks etc. If you get stood over once, it will happen every time you go to the Canteen.

Soured

Soured means you have been raped, either by another cunt or a screw. This happens routinely so be prepared. Condoms are provided for men but if you get soured – the condoms don't come with lube and it hurts.

Gobbie

In male prisons this means a blow job to either a screw or a cunt.

In female prisons this means a blow job to a male screw to receive favors in return.

And there are many more but if you start with these, you will at least appear that you know what you are doing and won't be stood over so quickly.

Chapter Three: Money

In Victoria, you are allowed to have a friend or family member give you $140 per month and another $50 to use the phone.

This is helpful because your pay is around $3 per day and one fifteen minute phone call, from phones that rarely work, can cost up to $20 per call in a scam between Corrections and Telstra who has the sole contract and charges interstate charges for landline calls which is technically illegal.

I am told that Women prisoners are only allowed six minutes and that their charges are even higher but have been unable to confirm that.

All prisons require you to work in order for you to earn your $3 per day, unless you have a reasonable medical reason as to why you can't work in which case you will earn just $1 per day.

This becomes very difficult when you first arrive because essentials such as deodorant, shavers, soap, shaving cream, shampoo are not provided and they cost a lot at the Canteen. So it can take weeks or months before you get a chance to be able to just have the basics.

When you finally get to a point where you can afford something like a can of Coke as a luxury, you've likely already been stood over several times.

Being stood over probably requires its own Chapter but essentially, the definition is pretty clear: if you are 'fresh meat' or a 'new cunt' then everything you purchase at the Canteen is up for grabs.

You save up enough to afford a watch and actually wear it, expect a bunch of cunts to surround you and say: "that's a nice watch, I'll be having that now". Complain to the screws and then you're a dog and you'll be stood over even more in the future and in larger numbers.

Showing strength in the Canteen line is paramount – it's one of the few areas of the prison that really can get you into trouble no matter how much you try to stay off the radar. Other cunts will watch what you are ordering, when and how and without access to the internet, SMS or any other form of modern communication available the rumor mill runs faster than the NBN.

Unless you want to stink, never shave, be eaten alive by mosquitos, never know the time, the Canteen is important and the screws use it as a weapon of control and the outsourced staff that manage the canteens and other programs enjoy their power over you even more than the screws.

Fights break out routinely in the Canteen queues; so it's wise to work out your timing and strategy about what you buy, when and also where you store what you purchased because anything of value can go missing and don't assume it was another inmate or cellie.

Once you are in a position to start buying cans of Coke or chocolate, be careful where you leave them. To give you an idea – one can of Coke equates to one or two days of work and the going rate for a gobbie is one can of Coke.

In fact, cans of soft-drink are the main form of currency in both male and female prisons. So, walking back to your cell with a slab makes you a target unless you are mates with the top cunt or are extremely strong yourself.

You may well think that essentials like a shaver, deodorant, pens, writing paper, nail clippers, haircuts, toothpaste are provided – they are not.

You will have to save up for them. The only things provided on arrival are a plastic toothbrush (no paste), your 'greens' uniform, sneakers, and one small piece of soap. Everything else you need you need to save up for and buy at the Canteen if you are lucky enough to be served before it closes.

Chapter Four: Food

Everyone outside of prison thinks that prisoners get well fed and too much so.

Well – that's not true at all. The food in Hospitals would be akin to the world's best restaurants compared to what you get in prison.

In the morning, you are welcome to make your own toast and are provided with milk, oats and jam. Peanut butter is a luxury item that you must purchase from the Canteen and hide in your cell. And, if you like vegemite, you can't even save up for it because one cunt decided to try to inject it (because of it's yeast base because he was a severe alcoholic) and therefore all cunts statewide are not allowed Vegemite.

One bad apple spoils the bunch but when it comes to prisons, one bad apple is an excuse to punish all of the apples. The more abuse of power the better.

Lunch is usually vegetables with some bread. There is no margarine, salad dressing and whilst some prisons are better than others in this regard, the standard is pretty low.

You might get a piece of fruit or a biscuit or if you're in a low to medium security prison where you have your own 'cottage' and can cook your own food with utensils bolted to the sink and you have good cellies that agree with your 'budget' for raw ingredients and one of you can cook as well as budget then you might just have better food, until you run out of your allocated budget and need to 'barter' with people who have the crappy food from the kitchen.

The only hot meal of the day is dinner, well not always, but mostly and many cunts work in the prison kitchen as one of the jobs you can do to earn your $3 per day. They are not very generous, have no spices, flavor or variety.

Salt and pepper is available if you pay for it at the Canteen, otherwise get ready for a world of bland and if you do buy your own salt, don't be surprised if it goes 'missing' and don't be surprised if it's not because of your cellies.

The screws do routine searches of every cell. You are not allowed to watch what they do and it is quite common that an item you've been saving up for months has suddenly just gone missing and you have no way of proving it because; again: you are not allowed to watch. Why – just for fun!

More on this later when we get stuck into drugs because the screws also use these windows of opportunity to slot cunts they don't like or, worse, make them do more time by calling the jacks in and saying, falsely, that you've been using drugs in your cell and threatening your parole (if eligible).

But before I digress into broader issues – if you have been told that food in prison is decent, you've heard incorrectly. I lost 28Kgs in ninety days on the bread and water diet and I wasn't heavy beforehand.

Despite a few exceptions, the food is rubbish and definitely has no flavor. This is all by design – to make your life utterly miserable.

Chapter Five: Drugs

OK – this is a whopper!

Whether or not you are going to prison for drug related offences – this is going to blow your mind.

Before I go on – I am not a judgmental person in anyway. If you can show me someone who's never made a mistake, I'll introduce you to Casper the Ghost. I've made plenty of mistakes and I'm not proud of them but I don't hide from them either.

I've never smoked, never used illicit drugs but I'm an alcoholic - the main reason I ended up in prison. My reasons for all that are too boring for you as the reader.

Unfortunately for me, alcohol is the one drug in prison that is really hard to get because it's liquid and heavy.

Getting cigarettes and drugs in is very simple – you just get a friend or family member who is allowed to visit you to transfer money into the bank account of a screw (you need to memorise their details because paperwork is not allowed during a visit). Once the money hits the screw's bank account then your cigarettes or drugs are delivered to you. Problem solved unless you create debts on the outside you can't repay which becomes a problem when you are finally released.

Drugs and cigarettes in prison do not come in via your visitors. Your visitors pay the corrupt screws on your behalf and then the screws bring it in.

If you are an addict and going to rack up debts whilst inside then I won't judge you but here are some things to think of:

(a) for any drug you want to buy from a screw, you will be charged 400% than the going price on the outside and that could bite you later on;

(b) if you 'attempt' to bring something in via a visit, your visitor will be caught and then banned from seeing you again;

(c) routine but so called: 'random' piss tests will see you in the Slot for throwing a "dirty";

(d) the Medical Officers will give you syringes and disinfectant but you are not allowed to tell the screws because they have a zero tolerance policy as long as your family are paying them – the med guys know that it goes on and they want you to be safe so if you are going to get into it whilst inside, you might think you can trust them but you can't and

> using nicotine patches to turn them into cigarettes might feed your habit but not only will you be stood over for them but the health risks are more serious than you could imagine! I've lobbied for a long time now that tobacco be allowed back into prisons or not (patches are not the answer).

> Almost all prisons offer methadone programs for cunts that are coming off drugs. Some go into the 'line' for pain relief because other than panadol and nurofen, there are no pain killers allowed, nor sleeping tablets or anything that could be of 'value' inside the prison.

> Methadone is good for you if you are coming down from a serious addiction but it's bad for your teeth and also is actually addictive.

Therefore – if you need it then take it but try to put a timeframe on it, especially if you are in for a long time. Don't come out without your teeth and addicted to a substitute drug because otherwise you will be straight back on the real gear as soon as you get out.

And – there is a system when it comes to the queue for methadone: the top cunt runs the order of who gets in first but, essentially, when you arrive you start at the back of the line each morning and will progress as others ahead of you are released.

Chapter Six: The Slot

For those whom have never been to prison, being "slotted" simply means having been sent to prison.

Actually, all prisons have separation cells that are referred to as 'slots' but are technically referred to as single isolation cells.

There are also a number of different slots. Some are for dogs and laggers, some are for serious violent offenders that can't be in mainstream and some are for psychiatric purposes but most are used for punishment for cunts whom have done a dirty or pissed off a screw, which is illegal but the screws do it anyway.

Some people prefer to be in the slot rather than be in mainstream because it's less dangerous but the reality is that you are stuck in a concrete cell with no TV, no access to books, no kettle, no access to the canteen, only one hour a day to walk outside in your own three meter by three meter 'run out', a one minute shower, phone calls only if you book in advance, box visits for friends and family (if you are lucky), water, bread and a warm microwaved dinner that will likely give you the runs.

Again, some people prefer isolation but if you have an active brain then being in the slot will do your head in. Most people that spend a prolonged amount of time in the slot quite literally go insane due to the pure lack of contact with others.

Your food and meds are delivered to you through a 'trap' – think US prison films but a concrete door rather than bars and windows.

It's a living Hell unless you really like your own company only, a concrete bed, no heating, no time to shave or shower and enjoy torture.

If you upset a screw then you can be slotted for no reason. You have no say. It's their decision and their decision alone.

Quite often, cunts who get themselves in trouble in mainstream who don't want to be 'seen' as wanting to be slotted will cause a situation whereby they have to be slotted and this is known as a "professional bail".

If you are going to stage something whereby you need to be separated for your own safety then be careful because you could end up back in mainstream and considered a crumb and you may well leave prison in a body bag or face years of facial reconstructive surgery.

Chapter Seven: Outside Access

Anyone who has not experienced prison in Australia, be it through contact or actually being inside, think that prisoners have it really easy – phone calls, mail, libraries, computers, great food etc.

Forget all of that.

You are about to enter a world where the phones don't work, if you can find one within the allocated time and then out of your 'salary' you will be charged up to $5 per minute to speak to a loved one.

Depending on your sentence period, you can expect that your mail and visitors will drop off. Getting mail in prison is gold for a cunt – access to family, friends or just the outside world.

All mail is screened by the 'intel' screws before you get to see it and this can take weeks.

If an approved visitor gives you a book or newspaper to read; that goes through the same process so don't hold your breath – by the time you get access to it, the newspaper is pretty irrelevant. And for external mail – well, you need to buy envelopes ($1 each – a day's salary) and then the stamps ($5 each which is illegal) and then they get posted via a mailbox which you have to leave the letter open so that it can be screened by 'intel' before it is sent out, which again can take weeks if not months.

> Christmas, birthdays, friends all silently retreat because they think you've given up on them but actually it's the system they have no insight into.

> This is probably the hardest part of the world you are about to enter. Family, friends, colleagues, children will all quickly walk away and the ones that don't will slowly give up and that's how the system is designed – to break you down.

> There is nothing in Corrections Victoria that is about "corrections" or "rehabilitation" – it is all about punishment, despite the law being simply lack of freedom.

> When you stop getting mail or access to the phone, try not to let it get you down because it's normal. This is why being slotted is not easy because at least in mainstream you have some social interaction, especially when your friends and family on the outside have given up on you.

Of course, some won't and some will visit you and go through their own terrible issues to just be there for you. Some will do it to set up debts you will need to pay down the track so if you are not very close to your visitor then be careful.

The horrible truth is that people have so little knowledge of how corrupt and dangerous prison Officers in Victoria are that they just assume that if you are in prison you must have a reason to be there even though that could not be farther from the truth.

When you get out, as I've experienced, don't expect a lot of sympathy from friends and family. The truth is irrelevant to them – you are an embarrassment to them and therefore rather than being there for you, many may never talk to you again.

A prison sentence follows you for life! Not just the CRN which means you can barely get work but the social view that if you've been to prison you MUST have done something wrong.

Chapter Eight: Pain

If you suffer from any form of serious pain, then get used to it because there are no opioids allowed in prison unless you pay for them via a corrupt screw at a massive premium.

As mentioned before there is no panadeine, there is nothing but panadol and nurofen (Ibuprofen) and prescription medications are allowed as long as they don't include opiates. It's not that you shouldn't be in pain, it's that it would cut off the 'market' for the corrupt screws.

My pain was managed through panadol and ibuprofen and as a result I now have serious kidney damage, so much so I may not live that long without a transplant.

Ibuprofen is an over-the-counter pain killer but no one tells you that you should not take it daily because it will damage your kidneys and certainly no medical officer in a prison – all of whom (bar one) didn't care at all.

I suffered through it without bribing any screws but I was only there for ninety days so I wouldn't judge any cunt that was in for so long who suffers from pain that needed to get some pain relief from any drug. I wouldn't judge you for that because it's not your fault, or mine, that legitimate prescription drugs are not allowed in prisons.

Chapter Nine: Sex

I don't know much about sex in women's prisons. I do know that there are routine assaults that occur in men's prisons between cunts and screws, there is plenty of consensual sex. Condoms are provided freely and if you can find a hiding place in between musters and work that is not covered by a camera, it is possible to have sex with another cunt.

In male prisons – the saying is that: "no one is gay in prison".

I was soured by one of the Screws but never voluntarily offered it to another cunt but I wasn't in for that long so I can empathise with the long termers that have lived without sex for so many months or years that any form of sex is better than no sex, even if it is with a man and your are not homosexual.

It's utterly plausible that even the most straight male or female would at some point need some intimate contact and Corrections know that which is why they hand out condoms in male prisons and other devices in women's prisons – mostly because it stops problems, problems that could escalate if sex didn't occur; even though: it's technically not allowed.

Having sex with one of the screws is probably safer than doing it with a cellie because they will then become used to it and want more and once you're locked in for the night you can't do much about it unless you are the one demanding it I suppose.

However, negotiating where and when to have sex with a screw is also dangerous because if you 'hang out' with a screw too often then you become a crumb and that's really not good and you will end up in the slot very quickly. So, like drug dealing with a screw, sex arrangements need to be handled very discretely and usually you should keep the top cunt informed in case something goes wrong.

Masturbating is a whole other issue. Male or female, you are going to want to masturbate from time to time and when you are sharing a shower, toilet mirror etc with other cellies then it can be very difficult to masturbate without making noise or a mess.

It's OK to ask your cellie, straight up, that you will need to masturbate and if that annoys him or her then you know where you stand. Usually, the response you will get is that they will not just agree but are happy to do it for you if you do it for them. Remember: any intimate contact is better than none and you are going to be locked in with one or more others for fourteen hours a day.

Obviously I know less about the female side but for men – if you come to an 'agreement' where you pull each other off then you can more easily tidy up the mess. If you are circumcised it's a bit more difficult but otherwise you can hold your sperm and use the toilet to dispose of it.

Remember, your privacy is gone so if you have to shit in front of others and be stripped searched regularly, having a wank in front of your cellie is really not that big a deal; relatively speaking.

Just put it out there and if you agree on it, then you can masturbate at anytime without being embarrassed. That doesn't mean you have to agree or be forced into doing it jointly but it's best to discuss it upfront.

Chapter Ten: Violence

Whether or not you are a VO or a SVO, in for unpaid fines, theft or white-collar crime, you are going to be thrown into the mix. Again, only sex offenders, most Aborigines and famous people are separated into different prisons or sections of the same prison.

For reasons that make no sense, Corrections believe it's a good idea to mix all cunts together so if you are strong, well built, fit, tall and used to violence you will be fine.

If you are not – you're in for a ride.

Assaults, fights, stabbings, murders – these are daily issues you will encounter. In my ninety days I saw three stabbings, two murders, elven punch ups and was personally raped by one of the Screws whist another was masturbating and ejaculated onto my back.

In prison, there is one good rule when it comes to fights: there is no such thing as a "shit go" – on the outside the rules around coward punches etc. do not apply. If you are threatened and need to defend yourself, it's acceptable to do whatever you need.

The screws are not there to help you (even though that's their job) so if you are scared and lag to a screw – you will be slotted for your own protection and when you get out of the slot you will be a crumb so will need to be moved to the protection section of the prison and be surrounded by sex offenders.

So – defend yourself! The screws will not assist so it's up to you. If you've never been in a fight before – follow the rules: "there is no such thing as a shit go" – kick the cunt in the balls, trip him up, get him on the ground and start whacking the shit out of him until there is an audience and then the screws will finally intervene. Again: never show weakness.

If you get stabbed, you will be treated so just deal with it because the cunt with the improvised weapon is going to the slot anyway. Then you will be interviewed by Police and you tell them nothing!

If you lag on the assailant you become a Crumb and that will cause more problems. You worry about that when you get out and not before.

One very import lesson on violence – if you feel that are you in real danger, enough to talk to a screw then they will ask you: "So – you feel for your safety?" That's one of their many traps because you will think they will slot the person that is threatening you but what happens you get slotted and when released back in to mainstream you are a lagging crumb.

Chapter Eleven: You Can Survive

This short book is not intended to assist the system by scaring people away from prison – as much as the system would love that. It's all about corruption.

You are about to enter into a world that is unwatched, not monitored, full of bribes, corruption and terror because no one cares about you – you're a prisoner so you deserve whatever you get, even if you are truly not guilty.

Loved ones will likely desert you. You have a reasonable chance of being beaten up or slotted and no one will care. You are just a cunt now and that's going to stay with you for the rest of your life. Your job opportunities will forever be limited, your family will turn on you so the good cunts you meet inside will help you and there are plenty of them.

Unless you are a SVO or sex Offender, you will cope (as weird as that sounds) if you are paradoxically friendly and cautious.

Again – in your first few days you must make it clear to ALL that you will not be stood over by anyone and find a way to develop a relationship with the Top Cunt.

Chapter Twelve: Parole

Forget it.

Parole is designed to make cunts play nicely while inside so that they will get parole. Sounds good but very few cunts get parole whether they deserve it or not.

The best thing for your mental health is to not think about your parole date, known as the: "earliest". Just assume that you are not going to get out on your earliest and you will be fine. If you get out around that date then consider it a gift.

I just received a letter from an inmate and now one of my closest friends who has been told his parole has been entirely denied so he has another seventeen months inside. I did ninety days and was suicidal.

If you are given a parole period then that's good but don't expect it to work out for you even if you are a model prisoner. To the outside world and the Adult Parole Board you are just a crook.

And sometimes, it might be better to be released without parole conditions so that you can just move on. In my case, I was kept captive by Corrections Geelong for months for reporting despite a short sentence with a straight release.

Chapter Thriteen: Getting out

If you have survived prison without serious injuries then you're now in for the shock of your life.

Corrections are going to hold you hostage, especially if you are lucky enough to be out on parole.

You can't leave your State. You have to report three days a week to Corrections. Centrelink give you a week's salary (based on an asset test) and then you get the fantastic ability to have to apply for jobs at the same time as having a CRN, having to report, in person (which is really handy when you need to work – if you can't find work).

Some cunts have never seen a smart phone, don't know how to buy a train ticket (in Victoria: a Myki Card) but are just dumped at the closest train station. And before you know it, they commit a crime just because prison at least provides some food and a roof over their heads and is better than being homeless.

Chapter Fourteen: Oversight

The contents of the chapters of this book are written with very minor policy views or opinions and that was one of my greatest challenges as a politician.

But in this section, I am allowing myself to vent on the issues that most readers may not contemplate but affect their lives very severely.

We've had Royal Commissions into religious child abuse, abuse of the 'stolen generation', greed into the finance sector and we are about to have a Royal Commission into abuses in aged care (well overdue) yet we have prisoners starving, being raped, being tortured and mostly by the Officers who are there to protect and look after the prisoners.

Despite my language herein, not all 'screws' are bad but the problems are systemic. It's OK to rape or torture a prisoner because no one cares about them and Ministers across Australia have literally no idea what's going on with people they are responsible for.

Corruption is rife.

Abuse is rife.

Depression is rife.

The phones don't work so why have them at all?

The mail rarely gets through.

Why put VO's and SVO's in mainstream with prisoners who are in for unpaid fines or white-collar crime? We separate sex offenders and Aboriginals so what's the difference – putting me into a world of violence when I could have been given a different sentence is a lifelong punishment.

I have nightmares every night. I vomit every morning and I was only there for three months. The lack of dignity is expected but my naivety was that it would be unpleasant but not inhumane.

The word "Corrections" is all about rehabilitation but the Departments of Corrections in this nation are about punishment, not correcting bad decisions.

Yet, all in all, the most significant issue is a lack of oversight. The reason why most people that have been in prison re-offend is that their record stays with them for life.

This needs to now be managed by Federal Government and not the States and Territories.

You do a crime, you do the time to repay your debt and that's that. If it follows you around forever then who will employ you? No one and that creates serious social issues.

And that doesn't even go to the fact that 30% of prisoners are not actually guilty but they get tortured anyway.

Prison must be the absolute last resort and only ever for SVO's.

To think that America has a better prison system than Australia makes me sick.

We are a generous and caring nation so why don't we rehabilitate rather than punish? Because it's not a priority. That's fine until you end up in prison for doing something you did or did not do.

Being sent to prison is the punishment because you lose all of your rights and freedoms. Yet, society believes that if you are in prison, there must be a reason and thus the Ministers turn a blind eye which allows those that run and work in Corrections to make it all about punishment.

Corrections Officers believe that they have a right to not just take away your freedoms but to punish you – physically, emotionally, sexually.

Why?

Because: no one is watching.

We care more for illegal immigrants than we do for our own prisoners. The term: "Corrections" ought be changed to: "Who cares".

There is nothing about rehabilitation in prisons in Australia. To think that the US, Scotland, New Zealand and Norway are all ahead of us in terms of rehabilitating criminals is a disgrace.

People make mistakes. Some, yes, do things deliberately and may never be rehabilitated but, as Australians, we should at least try. We're not talking about live sheep here – we're talking about human beings.

In my short experience, only about 3% of prisoners are actually a long-term risk to society. The rest could be dealt with very differently and the costs to society and the tax payer would be far lower.

I'm very lucky in that I had friends, family and a loving partner to come home to as well as networks in business so that I could attempt to find work but that's highly unusual. Every Government in Australia needs to look into this properly because it's a massive problem and hiding behind the fact that there are no votes in it eliminates the fact that it causes massive social problems.

I would dare any State Corrections Minister to visit a Prison and actually talk to the prisoners – not the Management or the Officers – the actual inmates and they would be horrified as to what goes on under their watch as custodians of prisoners. It's incredible, in the latin sense of the word.

Chapter Fifteen: Derryn Hinch

The former massive alcoholic but famous radio news presenter, Derryn Hinch, who was sentenced to home detention, not prison, for exposing sex offenders and then went on to become a Federal Senator is a disgrace.

Hinch's Party, the Justice Party, and his career has been based on taking advantage of the common view that prisoners are treated too well and criminals don't get enough time for their crimes.

In his statements, he talks about prison being like a hotel!

Well fed, great hot food, great Officers, pools, gyms, football games, working phones, no fights, minimal lock downs, strip searches only for visits, internet access. He wouldn't have a clue – none of that happens in prison.

I'd dare him to spend one night in a mainstream prison and see if he still thought prisoners have it easy. He'd lie of course but I can guarantee you that it would be the worst one night of his life and that's not just because he couldn't get an alcoholic drink.

I'm not the only one to have sprung him (in person at the Atlantic Restaurant at Crown Casino – let alone his Uber Driver incident where he fell out the car because he was so pissed) – this idiot got a liver transplant because he was famous! And, yet he's still a pisshead.

As I've mentioned, there are a handful of prisons that are referred to as 'protection from protection' – these prisons are reserved for famous people, police, Magistrates and anyone else that would be an easy target in mainstream but he didn't even experience that – he, before the laws in Victoria were changed, was detained at his house!

In my case, I would have thought I would have been sent to a protection prison but I was not quite famous enough and I wasn't a cop, Magistrate or sex offender.

Putting a 'jack' or a corrupt Magistrate in prison is a death sentence for them so they get famous status and qualify for such a custodial sentence.

Having not been inside one of these few prisons it's impossible to speak from personal experience but I can state, with absolute certainty, that Deryn Hinch has never spent one minute in an actual prison and his views that prison is "pleasant" makes him the biggest moron in the nation.

Yet, he was elected to the Federal Senate and a was a terrible Senator who spent most of his time at the Bar! Thank God the nation voted him out but he wants to return – clearly he is delusional.

Chapter Sixteen: Accommodation

If you are thinking this is going to be rough but reasonable – forget it!

The cells are tiny, there is not enough room for your belongings. The curtains don't work, the shower curtains (if you get one) fall off. If you are on a top bunk, there is no way to climb up and no barriers so if you fall out of bed you are going to land on a hard concrete floor.

The mirrors have all been scratched up by former cunts (I don't know why they would do that but they do).

If you are lucky enough to have a TV – it's a small plastic TV with limited channels and the cause of many fights because most cunts are not highly educated and like to watch cartoons so if you, like me, want to watch something more interesting like the news – you will be outnumbered and just have to live with it.

Chapter Seventeen: Summary

I've kept this book short because there is a lot to take in and if you need or want to know more you can always contact me. I am not a registered Lawyer, a registered Psychologist but I've been through what you are about to go through.

You will have panic attacks, you will almost certainly be beaten up at some point (usually over nothing), you will be treated as 'fresh meat' – someone who doesn't understand the rules and hierarchy of prisons and your instincts to trust the screws will get you into serious trouble.

Haircuts are not provided so you will have to save up for cans of coke to pay another cunt who has saved up for clippers so that you can pay him for a buzz cut – usually two cans of coke or chocolate.

Prison is supposed to be a punishment in that your freedoms are removed but the screws, an unwatched, unsupervised power unto themselves can and will do anything they like to physically, emotionally and sexually abuse you.

So - go in strong!

Keep your tears and fears to yourself.

Put on a show of confidence at all times. Be careful who you befriend but don't expect to be handed a user manual – there isn't one (in any Prison) so you will need to ask other cunts for information such as Canteen times, where you get your washing done, how to get toilet paper, how to change your 'greens' if they don't fit, which they never do, what times can you go to the library, what times can you use the gym, what are the rules over different sections etc.

When asking these questions, make out like you have not been to this particular prison – pretend that you've been inside before but just don't know this one and use the "Lingo" from that start of this book.

For example: "Hey Bro – do you know what the fucking canteen times are? I haven't been to this prison before!"

Even a shit cunt will answer that type of question and you just keep going until you know the system and have worked out who the top cunt is and take it from there.

Don't ask anyone what they're in for!

It's really tempting and if you're asked by your cellie or someone else then just say: "the usual shit" until you have worked out who you can trust. At first you trust no one. If a cunt asks why are you so boring – you respond: "Do we have a problem Cunt?" and they will, usually, tell you to fuck off but then leave you alone until you find your way.

If someone tells you what they're in for – the rules change: then you are allowed to respond. Unless you are a sex offender, you won't be judged.

This experience is going to be a living Hell – make no mistake about that. It's not your fault that the system is broken and no one cares about prisoners but that's how it is so it's going to be a daily battle to stay strong and it's exhausting. Even if you are a nice guy – act like you are the opposite and you will come out alive.

Trust your instincts and don't fall into traps. Read this book a hundred times a week and you will come out alive and with a chance of moving on.

The most exhausting part of being 'inside' is just trying to survive. So use your time in lock down to breath deeply, dream of the future and not worry about what might happen the next day.

Stay hygienic – being sick in prison is not easy because the outsourced "Correct Care" workers don't care about you at all so make sure your cell is always clean and if necessary, tell your cellie to fuck off to the Gym if he refuses to help with the cleaning.

Don't get into fights – lay low and just put up with the crap food and jobs you are assigned to.

If you become a winger like I was, you will end up spending a lot of time in the slot and being moved from prison to prison.

You will be OK!

And, if everyone you know turns against you – contact me and put me on your call list:

0412 765 178

It is now one of my lifetime goals to stand up for the rights of prisoners – not because some people should be in prison but because of the corruption and the lack of human rights provided to in-mates – guilty or not.

Get your friends of family to email me:

kurtreiter@mac.com

I will do all I can to assist, not legally but emotionally.

We all make mistakes for all sorts of reasons.

My wife cheated on me and made me believe my daughter was mine and she then moved to London with my daughter with one day's notice to be with the real father. After that, I made a lot of mistakes and ended up in prison.

It's not an excuse for my behavior but the system is broken and; again: Corrections Victoria is not about 'corrections' nor 'rehabilitation' – it's about punishment and that is illegal under both the International Human Rights Treaty Australia is a signatory to but also the Victorian Charter of Human Rights and Responsibilities Act.

I hope this short book prepares you and guilty or not I will continue the fight for prisoner rights.

Stay STRONG!

www.ingramcontent.com/pod-product-compliance
Lightning Source LLC
Chambersburg PA
CBHW072257170526
45158CB00003BA/1094